The Road to Mastery: The Smart Way to Begin, Continue, or Redirect Your Riding Journey

GREG WIDMAR

Copyright © Greg Widmar
All rights reserved.
First Edition, 2019.

No part of this publication may be reproduced without prior written permission from the Publisher.

Published by:
MotoJitsu, LLC
San Diego, CA 92169

ISBN: 978-1-086-57269-8
www.motojitsu.com

Back cover photo by Karen E Ott Photography

SPECIAL THANKS

Special thanks to Andy of Immortal Concepts Studios for creating an amazing cover image and to Keith of Yamaha Champions Riding School for your insights and showing me what's possible. Your selfless dedication is truly appreciated.

FOREWORD BY KEITH CULVER

I met Greg Widmar towards the outset of his quest for motorcycle riding and education enlightenment. Right about that time, he got completely hooked on taking every new class he could get his hands on, and I watched him transition to that more enlightened and well-rounded rider. The more classes he took, the more tools he put in his toolbox. More importantly, I watched him become an advocate for rider training.

In early 2019, I was happy to get Greg into our Yamaha Champions Riding School "ChampDay" class at the Streets of Willow and really enjoyed watching his lightbulb get even brighter and seeing him leave with more tools. To see the culmination of all of these tools from all of these classes mold Greg into his own voice via his online presence and now his second book is impressive. *The Road to Mastery* is an easy-to-read and easy-to-follow road map for anyone wishing to get into motorcycling the right way and grow within the sport. Anyone new to motorcycle riding would be wise to read this book and use it as a reference.

I read somewhere that only 20% of students taking the new rider courses stick around as lifetime motorcycle riders. If that is true, it means we lose 80% of them and having more people like Greg would surely lower that number. Rider-education enthusiasts cannot affect all the reasons for these losses. However, we can help in our little segment by educating riders to be safer. Safer riders have more fun and the best way to make safe riders is to make good riders. Good riders, who are safer and thus having more fun, will most likely stick around and be fellow riders for a longer time.

I am glad that Greg has joined the privileged group who wake up every day with a plan to make motorcycle riders better. I join him in encouraging all riders to continue their education with qualified expert instruction. We need more advocates like "Fast Eddie."

"Practice makes permanent not perfect." "The most important upgrade to the motorcycle is the rider." "I thought I had 10 years of riding experience and then I took a school and realized I had one year of riding experience…10 times." The dedicated instructors in our industry have all coined phrases like these and, who knows, maybe someday someone will include "Shut up and Practice" in this list of wisdom-inspired quotes.

Keith Culver
Chief Operating Officer, Yamaha Champions Riding School
Coaching Leader, United States Motorcycle Coaching Association

THE ROAD TO MASTERY

CONTENTS

Preface

1. Get Your License — 1
2. Motorcycle Gear — 5
3. Choosing a Motorcycle — 11
4. Practice — 17
5. Additional Courses — 21
6. The Brakes — 25
7. Mindset — 27
8. Giving Back — 29

PREFACE

This book is about the Road to Mastery. It isn't easy, and the majority of riders do not seek it. Most take the wide-open trail. It's clear, well lit, and inviting. There are signs to tell you which way to go, what to expect, and how many miles until your next rest stop. There are ropes and fences to keep you going in the right direction. The ground is well maintained, flat, and predictable. You can see what's ahead with few surprises to worry about. You can even look forward to restrooms and water fountains along the way for your convenience. Due to these features, it will feel as if this is the correct path to take. Don't be fooled.

The Road to Mastery isn't found on a wide-open trail. It's on a small path most people never notice, even though it's at the same starting point. Many people don't initially choose to start on the Road to Mastery. It usually takes a painful experience for them to wake up and realize that more gear, courses, and practice are required to ride safely on public roads. Years on the wide-open trail will only offer a false sense of security due to repeating basic techniques over and over again.

On the Road to Mastery, there are rocks and roots to trip you up. Steep hills and sharp boulders are scattered in every direction. The path seems to disappear every 20 feet, frequently causing you to second-guess where you're going. It's dimly lit with unpredictable footing at every step. There are no signs, markers, or directions to follow. For many riders, this path doesn't seem to be worth the trouble, but the Road to Mastery will give you tools not found anywhere else.

You will learn to be resilient and to adapt to an ever-changing environment—exactly what is needed to ride on the public roadways. You will be better equipped to respond to traffic, your judgment will sharpen, and the likelihood of you becoming another accident statistic will be lower. You will learn to not give up, how to go through hardships and setbacks, mistakes and disappointments and still move forward. You will learn to do whatever it takes to accomplish your goals. The thrill and pleasure of riding a motorcycle will be enhanced and the satisfaction gained from the experience will be priceless. This is the Road to Mastery.

CHAPTER 1

GET YOUR LICENSE

To begin, you'll need your motorcycle endorsement. In the United States, there is a variety of options for obtaining your license. The most preferred method is to take the approved basic course for your state. The other is to make an appointment with your local Department of Motor Vehicles (DMV) to set a date to take the written and riding evaluations. If you pursue this option, you will need to provide your own motorcycle and will be starting your riding career already going in the wrong direction—not a smart choice.

I recommend attending whichever formal course is available in your state before you obtain your license. The curricula are constantly being updated with better techniques, materials, and exercises to ensure that you get the most up-to-date information about motorcycle riding. The two, or more, days you spend with instructors will provide a solid foundation to build upon; if not, you'll resemble a person trying to build a home in the sand—it's not going to last. If you already have experience, some of the information may be a refresher. However, I guarantee that you will learn a lot more than you expect. Additionally, you will be provided one-on-one feedback while riding in order for you to understand what you're doing well and how to improve.

Some of the more popular courses for those with no experience in the United States are the Motorcycle Safety Foundation's "Basic RiderCourse," which can be found at msf-usa.org; California's Motorcyclist Safety Program's "Motorcyclist Training Course" at cmsp.msi5.com; and the "Total Control Beginner Riding Clinic" at totalcontroltraining.net. A simple Internet search can determine which course is available in your state.

If you already have riding experience and your own motorcycle but still want to attend a motorcycle course, many states in the U.S. offer a one-day course as a licensing waiver instead of the two-day basic course. This way, you will get feedback from instructors on your own motorcycle: win-win! In Texas, for example, completion of the "Total Control Intermediate Riding Clinic" results in the student earning his/her endorsement. For more information and to see if this course is available in your state, contact Total

Control Training, Inc., at totalcontroltraining.net.

Once you enroll in the appropriate course for you, the site will send you an email with key information to look over prior to starting. This will include directions to the course location, what to bring, what gear is required, policies on arriving late, your schedule, and so on. It's recommended that you read through all information and contact the staff with any questions you may have prior to the start date.

As you prepare for the class, be sure to find out what specific gear is needed and what is offered at the training site you're attending. Most courses provide a helmet on loan and the motorcycle to ride. As a general guideline, the following are examples of the minimum clothing required to ride: a long-sleeved shirt or motorcycle jacket; jeans without any holes, rips, or tears; street motorcycle gloves; and durable, sturdy boots.

If only a helmet is provided, you are responsible for everything else. If you're unsure of the requirements, contact the staff and get clarification. If you already have your own motorcycle gear, I recommend bringing it with you on day one so the instructor can approve it before the afternoon riding session begins.

While attending the course, be sure you're able to fully participate without any distractions or prior commitments. It's disappointing to see students cancelling due to not clearing their schedules fully. Most students in the class have zero experience on a motorcycle and will be nervous; this is 100% natural and expected. In order to help ease any apprehension, below is the overall layout of a basic two-day course in the United States.

One tip before we begin: if you already have a motorcycle, you may be able to use it in the course if it meets the requirements for the state's program. For example, in California you're allowed to use your own motorcycle if it meets two out of these three requirements: 400 pounds or less, 500cc or less, and 30-inch seat height or less. If this is an option you want to pursue, contact the staff prior to the start date to see if your bike qualifies.

Most beginner courses are two days and consist of a morning classroom session followed by riding in the afternoon. The classroom portion generally lasts two to three hours and feature an introduction to riding a motorcycle, expectations of the course, the risks of riding, proper motorcycle gear, the basic controls of a motorcycle, and so on. An instructor, usually with the aid of a PowerPoint presentation, will teach the classroom sessions.

Sometimes during the first classroom session students feel they're in over their heads, that it's going to be too difficult for them to learn and they won't successfully pass the course. They're afraid of dropping their bike or otherwise embarrassing themselves in front of their peers. It's normal to feel this way and more often than not, the light bulb will only come on at the end of the day after having time to ride the motorcycle and put the information into practice. In my experience as an instructor, however, as anxious as students may be in the beginning of the day, they can't stop smiling toward the end.

Once the classroom portion is completed, you will have time to get lunch before meeting up at the motorcycle range, which is a dedicated area to ride. The riding portion will last around three to four hours. Each state's beginner course is designed to teach someone with no experience on a motorcycle. The exercises start with very basic drills and slowly add more complicated ones. You will receive multiple breaks throughout the day to digest the information. Most training locations will ride rain or shine, so dress accordingly and bring necessary seasonal comfort items, such as sunglasses, sunblock, and warming layers.

At the end of the first day, you will likely have ridden 10 or more miles on a motorcycle! Congratulations! You're going to be comfortable getting on and off the bike, starting and stopping, changing gears, and basic turning in just a few hours. Keep in mind you will most likely be mentally drained and physically exhausted if you have no prior experience. The course is almost like drinking from a fire hose: lots of information thrown at you all at once. Before dismissal, I always remind students to eat a filling dinner, drink lots of water, and try to get a good night's sleep to prepare for day two.

Day two mirrors day one, with classroom time followed by riding in the afternoon. At the end of the second classroom session, you will have a written test covering the information taught on both days. This is a multiple-choice exam in which you must earn an 80% or higher to pass. If you've been paying attention, taking notes, and have participated during the presentations, you'll do fine. Most students pass the written test; the ones who do not are the ones who simply weren't paying attention.

After the classroom instruction, the riding portion will cover more in-depth riding techniques, including higher-speed cornering, emergency braking, low-speed control, and swerving. All of the classroom sessions and your previous day's riding will begin to make more and more sense, and there are often students saying, "Oh! That's what you meant yesterday— now I get it!" or "Wow, you weren't kidding! The clutch and turning your head really does make all the difference for doing that U-turn!" Comments like this are common on the range on day two.

I also want you to keep in mind that the course is limited by time constraints. Each exercise can only be practiced for so long before moving on. It may feel a bit rushed and you'll want so much more time to practice. Understand that the course will only give you the basic ideas of what you must practice on your own once you get your own bike. It's going to be up to you after the course to practice each technique until it's part of your muscle memory.

The course will conclude with a riding evaluation, which measures your ability to perform the techniques taught in the course. The test is one student at a time per exercise. There are usually five exercises to complete. The good news is there are no surprises at all during the exam. The drills you will be asked to perform are the exact same things you have been practicing up to that moment.

Many students get nervous and feel test anxiety, which is natural; if you happen to run over a cone or cross over a boundary, so be it. No one error by itself will cause you to fail the test—only a collection of errors will. Out of all the classes I've been teaching for the past four years, it is rare that anyone gets a perfect score; even the riders who have already been riding for many years make mistakes. What will hinder your performance, however, is beating yourself up over it after it happens and being unable to let it go. If you can, think of a mistake as a cloud passing by—no need to judge it or get upset about it, just let it drift on peacefully.

On the other end of the spectrum, I've seen students start swearing and yelling after making a mistake, punching the gas tank after running over a cone, and arguing with the instructors after crossing a boundary line, as if the instructors caused them to do what they did. You're the one riding the bike, correct? Taking responsibility for your actions is a sign of maturity. There's no need to worry about things you cannot control, and you can't go back and redo it.

If all the students pass the evaluation, I often say during the end-of-day debrief, "Congratulations everyone! You're all pretty good at riding 20 miles per hour in a parking lot! However, please do not think you have the skill, awareness, reflexes or knowledge to handle a motorcycle on the highway. Once you get your own motorcycle, practice riding around your neighborhood until all that was taught in this class becomes easy for you—*then get into an intermediate-level course.*" As you can imagine, this isn't the most popular thing to say, but it's necessary.

If you did not pass the riding evaluation, more practice is needed. Everyone learns at different rates, and oftentimes students who fail the first time around improve dramatically the second time due to already knowing what to expect and from having additional riding time. You probably will not have to repeat the entire two-day course either—maybe just the riding portion from the second day. Your instructor will tell you your options before you leave for the day.

CHAPTER 2

MOTORCYCLE GEAR

Before you start searching for your dream bike and practicing, it's time to go shopping for proper motorcycle gear—the only protection you have while riding. No matter what kind of bike you're looking for, where you will be riding or how often, purchasing high-quality riding gear is your next smart investment.

On a motorcycle, you have no protection. There are no crash bars or airbags, no seatbelts or crumple zones to offer shelter like in a car. Your only defense is what you put on your body. To demonstrate how important gear is, I invite you to participate in this thought experiment. Put on all the gear you're planning to ride with and drive to your nearest highway in your car. Once you get to 65 miles per hour, imagine opening the door and jumping out. That's what it's going to be like to crash on a motorcycle. The tumbling, sliding, and impact you're going to absorb is extensive. The trauma will only increase if you collide with another vehicle or a stationary object like a guardrail or tree. The need for full, quality gear is literally a matter of life and death. A popular saying among knowledgeable motorcyclists is "All gear all the time," or simply AGATT. Since accidents don't happen only when you're ready for them, the constant need to be protected is obvious.

Wearing motorcycle gear is a personal choice; some riders wear only the bare minimum, and others are in full gear no matter what. In California the only requirement is a helmet approved by the Department of Transportation (DOT). I recently saw a rider wearing a tank top, shorts, no gloves, and flip-flops while riding down the interstate. To each their own, I suppose.

When I see riders who choose not to wear protective gear, I just look at it as a good example of what not do to. Most likely those riders have never been in a crash, because the consequences would keep them from taking such risks. It's your choice; however, if you take a few minutes to consider what you're risking, there's only one smart decision to make: ride in full, quality gear each and every time you get onto a motorcycle.

No matter the cost, quality gear will always be less than hospital bills. Save your money and keep upgrading your gear until you're satisfied with your level of protection. The first purchase I recommend is a high-quality helmet.

Helmets: The most important piece of gear you can purchase is a helmet. Like anything else in life, you get what you pay for. Not all helmets are the same and there are various considerations to keep in mind when shopping for one. The most obvious is the amount of protection it provides. A full-face helmet provides the best protection because of its coverage of the entire head and face. This is what I recommend all riders wear, regardless of where they ride, what they ride, or how often they ride.

A bit lower on the protection scale are three quarter or open face helmets, where the head is protected but the face is open, leaving your face and chin exposed to the elements. With this type of helmet, even a bug hitting your face is going to hurt, never mind the pavement during a crash. I once had a bird hit me in the face at 60 miles per hour; anything less than a full-face helmet would have been devastating.

The least amount of protection you can get for a helmet is a half helmet. Your head isn't fully covered and there is no protection for your face. This helmet is most likely to come off during a crash and is almost worthless in providing protection for your brain. If you look at the location of most impacts during a crash, you will see the chin area to be the highest (motorbikewriter.com/crash-statistics-motorcycle-helmets). Additionally, most crashes involve multiple impacts to the helmet—not just one. Be smart: get a full-faced helmet and wear it every time you ride.

In order to determine how much protection your helmet will provide, check the helmet's certifications. The legal standard for motorcycle riders in many states is a DOT-approved helmet. What's important to remember is DOT does not test the helmet—it relies on the manufacturer to do any testing or send it to a third party to have it tested. I encourage you to research the current certifications including ECE, SNELL, and FIM in depth to learn about the testing procedures and standards each one has in order to make an informed decision.

If you want a helmet that provides the highest protection possible using the most realistic testing procedures, research 6D Helmets (6dhelmets.com). My helmet is a 6D ATS-1, and the peace of mind I have knowing I have the best in helmet safety technology was worth the money. The technology inside this helmet is so impressive that I even made a YouTube video about it.

Other features to consider when shopping for a helmet are size, color, airflow, weight, etc. Of course, these should all be secondary once you get one that will protect your head in case of a crash. Most companies have slightly different shapes for their helmets, so your size may fluctuate from brand to brand. The best practice is to try on the helmet in a store and walk around with it on for about 15 minutes. This way, you'll be able to tell if there are any hot spots or acute pressure points on your head, which indicate the helmet is too small or the wrong shape for your head. If you find a helmet that seems to fit, check with a sales representative to ensure it's indeed the right choice.

Additionally, consider which colors are most visible for drivers to see. Bright colors and eye-catching designs will make you more likely to be seen out in traffic. You can also add reflective stickers to your helmet if you ride during early morning hours or at night. 3M Reflective Tape is a popular brand among motorcyclists and is available everywhere.

Jackets and Pants: These two pieces of gear are the bread and butter of your protection because they cover the majority of your body. I recommend making sure the jacket and pants you consider have the capability to add armor in the areas of the body most likely to be injured in a crash. Motorcycle armor is made up of padded inserts to help absorb an impact to your joints and bones. Think back to the 65 mile per hour leap from your car: where are the areas you will want to have protective armor to absorb those impacts? At minimum, I encourage you to get armor in the elbows, shoulders, back, hips, and knees. Most jackets and pants only have a layer of comfort foam in those areas, which won't do much for you in a crash.

When you're checking out a jacket or pair of riding pants, look inside and check if there is any armor in it. If there is not the capability to insert any armor, I would move on. If there is, remove that armor and see if it's comfort foam or actually has some strength to it. Ask a sales representative to help you out if needed. I recommend buying CE-approved armor like D3O or equivalent.

CE is the abbreviation of the French phrase Conformité Européene, which means "European Conformity." This is the motorcycle safety standard for European gear. America has unofficially adopted these standards, but the law for street use does not require them. To ride a motorcycle in Europe, for example, you have to have protective gear that meets these standards. For the best quality of armor, look for CE Level 2.

I have D3O Level 2 armor in all my riding gear. The confidence I have in this armor is a result of having multiple crashes and walking away totally intact with not even a bruise afterwards. Ensure the gear you have either comes with high-quality armor already inside it or upgrade what's already there.

The material your jacket and pants are made of is an important factor when deciding what to buy as well. If your jacket is made of thin, cheap material, it's most likely not going to hold up from a slide across the pavement. You're going to want abrasion-resistant material. Certain leathers, as well as man-made materials, can provide comfort and safety. With both options, there are various levels of quality of protection.

For example, there's cow, deer, elk, and kangaroo leather for animal hide and man-made material such as Cordura and Kevlar. I used to ride with a leather jacket but the limited ventilation and comfort while teaching prompted me to switch to other materials. I recently purchased Klim's Carlsbad jacket and K Fifty 1 Riding Jeans due to the practicality, protection, and overall quality (klim.com). This gear is not only well-vented but also comes with D3O armor already in it. Shop around and try on various brands and styles until you're happy with what you're paying for. Go to motorcycle dealerships or motorcycle attire-specific stores in order to have a large selection to choose from. Another great resource for motorcycle gear and parts is revzilla.com.

When trying on your gear, a trick I've learned is sitting on a motorcycle of a similar type to the one you have or are looking to buy in order to see how comfortable it is going to be in a riding position. Just standing up and walking around in the jacket and pants won't give you a clear gauge of how it will fit while on the bike. At a minimum, sit in a chair with your jacket and pants on to feel if the gear is comfortable and if the armor in it is in the locations it's supposed to be in. This will give you better insight when making your selections.

Boots: When choosing boots to purchase, an easy method to narrow down quality versus low-grade is to consider if the boot was made for riding a motorcycle in the first place. Fashion boots, cowboy boots, and basketball shoes were never designed to protect your feet and ankles in a motorcycle crash. Most quality motorcycle boots go over your ankle, are very sturdy, and provide a non-slip sole. Quality boots also protect your feet from the heat of the engine and any objects that may fly up and strike you.

To determine if your boot is sturdy, hold it from the bottom with one hand and see how much effort it takes to fold it in half with the other. If you can easily bend it in half, it's not going to provide you with much protection. There should be some rigidity to the boot and added protection for your feet and ankles. Many boots have toe sliders, zippers, and clasps to ensure a tight fit, and Velcro for added security and ease in getting the boot on and off.

When you're picking out a boot, the focus should be adequate protection and enough flexibility to shift gears and easily operate the rear brake lever. If there are shoestrings on your boots, always tuck them into your boot in order to prevent them from getting caught in the chain, belt, or sprocket. If the boots you're looking at go above your ankle, bring your riding pants with you when trying them on to ensure your pants will go over the top of them. Shop around and try on a variety of boots before making your choice. You will see very quickly why some boots cost $60 and others $460.

I have Alpinestars SMX 6 v2 Boots, which I wear for both street and track riding. The protection, comfort, and style are why I've bought this same boot numerous times.

Gloves: If you're walking down the sidewalk and trip and fall, the first thing most people will do is put out their hands to brace themselves. In a crash, there's no time to think about where to place your hands in order to minimize damage—you're going to rely on the gloves you have to protect you. When purchasing gloves, make sure they're made for riding a motorcycle. Baseball batting gloves, mechanic's gloves, or fashion leather gloves will not hold up in a crash. There are some gloves that offer great protection without sacrificing comfort. After going through many pairs of gloves that did not provide both, I came across Sumo and Sumo R gloves by Lee Parks (leeparksdesign.com). They offer high-level protection and are very comfortable; I have been riding with Lee's gloves for the past three years now. I also have a pair of Dainese 4 Stroke Long Gloves that are a great value.

Most people who start riding will buy a helmet, jacket, and gloves. I didn't get riding pants for at least three months after I started riding until I took another course and was required to have riding pants in order to participate. I'm very lucky nothing happened in those three months because the jeans I was wearing wouldn't have helped me in a crash. Oftentimes, luck or hope is relied upon for those riders on the easy wide-open trail—those on the Road to Mastery know better.

Since I started riding, I have gone through five helmets, multiple jackets and pairs of pants, at least eight pairs of gloves, and so many pairs of boots that I've lost count. One jacket I bought lasted only a month before the stitching and zippers started to come apart. Another jacket I wore for more than two years before giving it away, and it lasted the recipient an additional two years without any issues. The first jacket was $130, the other $399. I've had some gloves last a month, and others an entire riding season.

Cheap is the low-hanging fruit dangling above the easy path where many riders find themselves. Quality gear is more expensive but will protect you far better in an accident. I know riders who buy a new pair of shoes each month to add to their collection yet tell me they don't have the money for stronger boots. Another rider goes out to lunch every day but complains about not having enough money for quality gloves. Take time to reflect upon what's important to you and where your money is going before making excuses about riding gear.

With this information, I hope you have the knowledge to distinguish between cheap and quality riding gear. Of course, each one of these topics can be discussed for hours on end and there is so much information available. However, be careful not to rely solely on the salesperson or opinions of others to determine what your level of protection should be. A great resource of reliable information is the book *Total Control*, 2nd Edition, by Lee Parks. An entire chapter is dedicated to motorcycle gear with insight that cannot be found anywhere else.

Now that you're in better position to know how to pick out quality gear, the next step is choosing a motorcycle. The motorcycle you decide upon should be able to help you fulfill your goals, not limit them.

CHAPTER 3

CHOOSING A MOTORCYCLE

A common question I get is, "What's a good beginner bike?" Without any other information about the rider's goals, size, weight, and experience, it's almost impossible to give much insight. However, I don't believe there is such a thing as a beginner bike, only beginner riders. If you're a really good rider, you can take any motorcycle and ride it very well, but if you're a new rider, no matter which bike you have you will not be able to ride it to anywhere near its capabilities. What someone would describe as a beginner bike might be someone else's dream bike, perfectly capable of fulfilling his or her goals. To help navigate through what to get, here's some insight I've learned after buying and trading in numerous motorcycles over the past six years.

As a general guideline, choose a bike that's comfortable, meets your needs, and isn't too heavy for your size and strength. I recommend getting a bike with less than a 500cc engine for at least the first year of riding. This way, you'll have time to learn the proper techniques and get used to riding on public roads on a bike that isn't too powerful or heavy. The Road to Mastery will be that much more challenging if you're trying to navigate the terrain carrying a 35-pound tent versus a five-pound tent. Going too big too soon is what often gets riders into trouble.

I highly recommend taking an additional motorcycle course on your new bike once you're comfortable enough on public roads to get to the training site. You will see with higher-level training that it's the not the bike that's limiting your abilities—it's you. The better you get, the better the bike will perform. This does not mean the bike will change in any way physically, but your ability to unlock the potential within the bike will grow and your journey will be that much easier.

Many riders you find on the wide-open path will blame the bike for everything; you will hear them say it's the bike's fault that they're slow or it's the bike that's limiting their ability to be able to do a U-turn. Those on the Road to Mastery understand it's the rider who is the limiting factor, never the bike. Keep upgrading the software (your skill); the hardware (your bike) is just fine.

For the last two years, my daily rider was a 2016 BMW R1200 GS, a big adventure bike. I would frequently go on long trips, take the bike to the racetrack, ride on- and off-road, carry luggage and passengers, and commute to and from work. I needed a bike that could do it all. The 1200 GS has been described as a Swiss Army knife due to its wide-ranging capabilities.

I recently traded in that bike since my goals have shifted and my focus is now in a different direction. No longer am I traveling long distances or have the need to carry large amounts of luggage. The big adventure bike was no longer fulfilling my needs and the new bike is better able to meet the aspirations I have. I highly encourage you to deeply consider what you're going to be doing with your motorcycle so you can make the best choice possible.

My first motorcycle was a 2012 Honda CBR 1000 RR. That is like buying a Lamborghini Diablo as your first car—not the smartest choice in the world, I admit. I quickly realized I felt as if I was wasting the bike's time due to my woeful inability to handle the size, weight, and power of it. I was happily ignorant and cruising down the easy path surrounded by likeminded riders, completely unaware of the Road to Mastery.

As you're shopping for a motorcycle, visit multiple dealerships around your city and sit on the bikes you're curious about. See what's interesting to you. Discover what's comfortable and what's not. Take a picture of the bikes you like and research them. Watch videos of people who already own that model and listen to their opinions. Watch reviews of the bike you're looking into—they are often very helpful.

Find out when a motorcycle store or dealership is hosting a motorcycle event like a bike night. Bike nights are public gatherings of riders and usually the hosts offer free food and entertainment. (I recently went to a bike night that Cycle Gear hosts once a month. There must have been more than 50 motorcycles there.) Walk around and chat with people. If you find someone with a bike that's similar to what you're looking to get, ask about the pros and cons, the reasons they choose it, how long they've owned it, and any issues they've had with it. What are the bike's features? Does it have a fuel gauge? (You'd be surprised at how many don't). What type of technology is in it? Where did they buy it? Ask if there is a salesperson they recommend at a specific store. Interacting with other riders is one of the best things about joining the culture of motorcycle riders; everyone loves to talk about their bikes and can usually offer helpful insight.

Looking back on the first bike I bought, I realize now I bought it due to the pressure of other riders I knew. They all had powerful sport bikes and I felt I had to get one as well. I wanted to fit in. I wanted to be accepted and perceived as one of the guys. Over the years of trial and error and thousands of dollars selling and trading in previous bikes, I finally started to think about a bike that would fulfill my needs, not whether others would approve of it.

The first variable to consider is what you are going to do with this bike. Only commute to and from work? Ride on the weekends? Go on long-distance road trips? Explore the dirt trails around your neighborhood? Track days? The more realistic you can be with yourself, the better your choice will be. If you know you're only going to ride to and from work, get a bike that's lightweight, inexpensive, and comfortable. There's no need to spend $10,000 on a motorcycle that's ridden less than an hour a day.

While you're doing your research, consider what type of bike you're interested in. Do you like the look of a sport bike but are unsure of the comfort it provides? Do you want the relaxed sitting position of a cruiser? Would you rather be sitting in a neutral position and are looking for an upright bike? Are you completely lost and have no idea what I'm talking about? The more homework you do, the more you will start to understand the various types of bikes there are and start to get a picture of what's best for you. If you are considering a sport bike I personally recommend borrowing or renting one first in order to see and feel the limitations during street riding.

In your search, if you discover certain options you know you're going to want, write them down or make a note in your phone about them. I have met so many people who bought a bike they never planned on getting because the salesperson persuaded them to buy it. If you want a bike with a fuel gauge so you don't have to guess when you need to fill up, be sure to have one. Do you want the bike to indicate what gear you're in? Make sure it has that option. Anti-lock brakes? Check. What you don't want to happen is a month after you purchase the bike you discover other motorcycles you weren't aware of with more of what you originally wanted. One of the best negotiating tools you possess is the ability to walk away after speaking to a salesperson. Don't get talked into a purchase or price you're not willing to live with. Take your time, shop around, and do your research.

If you're like me and want to test ride a motorcycle before buying it, you will be disappointed to learn only a few dealerships allow this. BMW and Harley Davidson are the only two that I know of, and even this varies from location to location. The good news is there are other options. I recently discovered a website where you can rent someone's personal motorcycle for the day, giving you the opportunity to try out various types of motorcycles before committing to a purchase. The website is twistedroad.com, and I know many people who have used it so far without any issues. In addition, various motorcycle dealerships often have demo days. This is where motorcycle manufacturers provide the latest models to test ride.

An additional resource I recommend is Club Eagle Rider. This is a program where you can rent various types of motorcycles throughout the

United States for minimal cost. If you're looking for a fun weekend with a street or dirt bike, or wanting to try different types of motorcycles before making a purchase decision, check out eaglerider.com.

One of the biggest variables to consider once you've narrowed down the type of bike and the options you want is the cost. What is your price range? Are you paying cash or financing it? What is the most you're willing to pay monthly? The more time you take into the planning, the less likely you will feel pressured into getting a bike you can't afford.

If you buy a new bike, you'll have a warranty and a safety blanket in case something goes wrong with the bike. Some offer an additional extended warranty, which I recommend getting. On my new motorcycle, a 2018 BMW S1000R, I added the additional warranty: six years and unlimited miles on the entire bike except for items that wear out naturally like tires and brakes. This also came with towing and roadside assistance—quite the deal. Additionally, I bought the previous year's model, so I got an awesome price on it.

Once you pick out a motorcycle that best fits your needs, I highly encourage you to get full insurance. Call your insurance provider and ask about the details. What options are available with your full coverage? Is motorcycle towing included? Is it an option? If you take additional motorcycle courses, will they give you a discount? If your insurance company has limited options, try another one. Shop around. See who is willing to give you the best protection for your price range.

If you're looking to get a used bike, I recommend taking along someone who has a lot of experience and can help you determine if the asking price is worth it and pitch in during any negotiations. Has the bike ever been in a crash or been dropped? What was damaged? Where was it fixed? Does the owner have the title? If they still owe on it, how much? Is there a warranty on the bike? If yes, how long until it expires and is it transferable? Ask for the receipts of every service that was done on the bike. If they don't have them, ask them to go to the shop where the work was done and print them off. If they did the service themselves, ask for the mileage of when it was done.

Check out the age of the tires. Tires start to go bad just like a banana sitting on your kitchen table. To understand why, imagine a brand-new pack of No. 2 pencils; what are the erasers like? They're soft, pliable, and fresh. If you placed that same pack of new pencils into a storage unit for five years and then took them out, what are the erasers like now? Hard, brittle, and can fall apart. Tires are the same way.

To check the age of the tires, look on the sidewall of the tire and find four numbers inside of an oval after the letters DOT. This is the tire's age. The first two numbers indicate the week the tire was made. The second two numbers represent the year. For example, the numbers 4317 would indicate the tire was made during the 43rd week of 2017. If the tires are more than a few years old, ask the owner to lower the price by a few hundred dollars to compensate for your having to replace them.

If the bike has a chain, inspect it. See if there's rust or deformities on it and whether it's the original or a replacement. Check the tension to see if it's too loose or tight. Check the sprockets to see if they're worn down, rusted, or bent, and if they have been replaced. If the bike has a belt instead of a chain, feel the tension of it and look for any imperfections.

Make sure all the lights work. Turn on the high beams. Check to see if the brake lights turn on after applying both the front and rear brake levers. Activate the turn signals; all four should light up and flash properly. Start the engine and listen for anything knocking or for excessive rattling. Take if for a test ride or have the person with more experience than you ride it. Feel the brakes out. See if there's anything off about the way it handles. Is it jerky? Pulling to one side? Wobbling? Making strange noises? Are the handlebars straight or is one side bent more than the other? This could be a sign the bike was dropped on that side.

After the test ride, leave it running for a few minutes to ensure the radiator fan kicks on if the bike is liquid cooled. Look to see if the brake pads are worn down. See if there's any sign of fluids leaking. Ask if the bike has ever had a leak, and if so where? What did the owner do to resolve it? And when?

If the bike has any aftermarket parts, like a new exhaust or different mirrors, ask if the originals are available, when the purchases were made, and who installed them. Sometimes, if the work was done outside a motorcycle shop, it may not have been installed correctly or may have been done poorly. The more you ask, the better you'll be able to make an informed decision on whether or not the bike is worth the asking price.

Since you now have full, quality gear and your motorcycle, there are a few things I recommend purchasing before taking your bike on public roads. First, protect the bike. Bike parts get very expensive very quickly if damaged. Depending on your type of bike, you will want to get frame sliders or crash bars in case of a tip over. These are made of metal or hard plastic that slightly stick out around the sides of the bike to prevent the motorcycle from hitting the ground. I would consider putting some type of wind deflector on your bike if it does not come with one already; riding with the wind blasting you in the face and chest isn't too comfortable, especially at faster speeds.

If your hands are small, change out your levers to make the clutch and front brake easier to operate. If your mirrors are too small or do not allow you to see much of what's behind you, get new, larger ones. The same goes for the seat—not many are comfortable and some mimic the feeling of sitting on an ironing board. Those can be changed out easily.

If you're going to carry luggage with you while riding, invest in some type of storage for it: saddlebags, a tank bag, or top case. Many options can be found for your bike at revzilla.com, among other online stores. Anything beyond what I've mentioned may be beneficial to you, but these are the bare minimum parts I recommend. Protect the bike, ensure the levers can be easily reached, and if you ride on the highways, get some sort of wind protection.

CHAPTER 4

PRACTICE

Many riders believe the key to improvement is simply riding more, getting more miles under their belt. This is a myth. Simply riding more is not the same as practicing. Practicing is focused attention to a specific skill through repetition. Most of us have heard the saying, "Practice makes perfect," but this is incorrect. Perfect practice makes perfect. I know many riders who are really good at the wrong thing.

One of the most common questions I get from people on my YouTube channel is how to improve their riding skills, as if there's a secret only I know about. There isn't. If you want to improve, attend higher-level motorcycle courses and spend time practicing what you learn. The idea is to practice so much that it's hard to make a mistake. This isn't what riders want to hear. It seems many riders I interact with want some kind of a microwave technique, something that's fast and easy yet yields the results they're looking for. There are no shortcuts to becoming a skilled rider. If you don't put in the time, you won't get the results.

If a car pulls out in front of you, you will not have time to think about how to stop as fast as possible—you will just react. Your reaction could be many things, but unless you burned the correct technique into muscle memory through repetition, you're unlikely to avoid the accident. To put it another way, without practicing, you are setting yourself up for failure. Just like it's said in the movie "Man on Fire": "There is trained and untrained. Now which are you?"

No matter your skill or experience, make time to practice at least twice a week. If there is one thing that separates me from most other riders, it is the amount of time I spend practicing the techniques I have learned in the courses I have attended. All motorcycle skills are perishable. Making time to practice will not only prepare you for the inevitable car coming into your lane or a distracted driver blowing through a stop light, but will also increase your confidence in yourself and the motorcycle's capabilities.

While you're practicing, accept and expect mistakes to happen. You may drop the bike during an attempted U-turn or skid the tire while stopping. Every rider goes through this period where it seems you can't do anything right, but what you do afterwards makes all the difference. Will you give up and stop practicing or will you look at the mistake you made as a great example of what not to do again? Your choice.

I spend hours each week practicing, repetition after repetition, seeing how I can improve. I try to figure out how to make the skill I'm working on even easier, and how to be more efficient and more relaxed while doing it. Many people over the years have seen what I can do on my motorcycle and tell me they wish they could do that. I tell them to stop wishing and make it happen. If you practiced playing the piano an hour every day, you're going to be pretty good in a month. Where will you be six months from now if you practiced a few times a week?

I hold free practice sessions once a week here in San Diego for anyone who wishes to join. We practice emergency braking procedures, slow speed maneuvers, cornering techniques, going over obstacles, trail braking, and so on. I do this to not only help others improve, but also to lead by example. When other riders see me putting in the time to practice and help others, they're inspired to do the same.

In addition to practicing, when you're just starting out I recommend taking it slow. Do not let others pressure you into doing anything you're not ready for or riding faster than what you're comfortable with. I see and hear about it too often: riders are out on the twisty mountain roads or taking long road trips with friends and are moments away from having an anxiety attack.

When you get your bike, start by exploring your neighborhood. Go around the block, then two, then three. Feel how sensitive the throttle and brakes are. Get used to having cars in front of or behind you. See how drivers respond to you and how they treat stop signs and stop lights. Practice using your turn signals and looking straight ahead while stopping and checking your mirrors frequently. How does the bike feel when turning? Listen to the sound of your bike when accelerating. And so on.

As you gain confidence and get more proficient, start to venture away from your neighborhood. Go for a 20- or 30-minute ride. Be aware of where you are and other drivers around you. Have an escape route while riding. If something unforeseen were to happen, what are your options? Can you slow down or stop? Should you swerve into another lane or is the best option to accelerate? Street riding comes down to having good judgement and never letting yourself get into a sketchy situation.

No matter the skill level or experience, what you're practicing, or where, there is one tip I always end up emphasizing: always move your hands very slowly. The slower you move your hands, the smoother a bike will respond. If you move your hands as if in slow motion when operating the clutch, throttle, and front brake, the bike will never surprise you. Your experience will be confidence inspiring and the bike will behave in a predictable fashion. You never want to do anything rapid with the controls. No stabbing or grabbing the brakes, no wrenching on the throttle quickly or releasing the clutch too abruptly. The faster you move your hands, the faster the bike will react. These actions tend to drain your confidence and could have you starting to fear the motorcycle.

To help you visualize this, imagine each control on the motorcycle as a light switch. Not an on/off light switch, but a dimmer switch. You want to practice using the throttle and brakes with slow, easy inputs—nothing quick or jerky. Slowly apply the brakes and slowly let off the brakes, slowly twist the throttle and just as slowly roll back off it. Having your hands behave like a dimmer switch will increase your overall satisfaction and experience while riding. Each input you do should be smooth, precise, and intentional.

A great place to practice your technique is in a local parking lot. I have been practicing in parking lots since I started riding. More often than not, riders and students who just passed the basic course will ask me what they should practice. My answer is all the things that you learned in the courses you've taken. As the years went on, more people asked me what they could practice and I became motivated to come up with a set of drills you can set up and practice on your own with minimal equipment needed.

Last year I introduced MotoJitsu, an easy-to-use but challenging program to help riders of all levels sharpen their skills and increase their knowledge of motorcycling. All you need is an empty parking lot, small cones (leeparksdesign.com/cones) or sidewalk chalk, and a tape measure. The heart of MotoJitsu is the belt system, similar to those used in martial arts. Each belt color represents a different level of knowledge and skill demonstrated by the practitioner. The system was inspired by my own experience of practicing jiu-jitsu and realizing the amazing abilities black belts possess in their understanding and knowledge. The MotoJitsu belt system mimics most martial arts by starting at White Belt and moving up to Black Belt and beyond. The skills and knowledge you are asked to explain and perform at the White Belt are at a beginner's level. As you progress, both get more challenging. For more information, check out my book *MotoJitsu Master Riding Program*, available on Amazon.

MotoJitsu can be set up in minutes and is very fun to practice. All of the drills are demonstrated on my website, motojitsu.com. Like anything else, in order to become proficient, it really comes down to the amount of time you're willing to practice. I practice MotoJitsu weekly with friends here in San Diego and I frequently travel to meet up with others wanting to practice. I'm happy to say that at this time I have sold around 3,000 copies in more than 20 countries. There are riders all around the globe who are finding MotoJitsu to be fun, challenging, and helpful, no matter what type of bike they ride or environment they're in.

MotoJitsu answers the question of what to practice in between formal training. In the words of Lee Parks, President of Total Control Training, Inc., who wrote the foreword to the book, "It is a clever framework under which any rider can build upon the skills they already possess before going back for more formalized training. I sincerely hope that this tool encourages riders everywhere to shut up and practice!"

CHAPTER 5

ADDITIONAL COURSES

As a newer rider, you will quickly start to meet other motorcyclists and will be given lots of advice. However, since you're just starting out, one thing to keep in mind is you're not going to have the knowledge or experience to know what's good or bad advice. Most people make the mistake of automatically assuming that just because someone has been riding for 20 years or has 500,000 miles of experience that he or she automatically is a very good rider. That person may have only taken the basic course to get their license and have been repeating the same basic maneuvers for 20 years. To get to a mastery-level understanding and riding proficiency, additional courses are required along with a substantial amount of dedicated practice.

Think of the basic course as an eighth-grade education. You're only introduced to the very basics of riding. If you want to deepen your understanding and riding ability, the next level of training would be like a high school education. I am confident that after that, you're going to want to earn the motorcycling equivalent of your associate degree, then bachelor's and master's. And it is hoped you'll continue on to get your doctorate degree. After you take an advanced course, it's your responsibility to take the initiative and spend time practicing what you've learned in order for it all to become automatic.

Here are a few advanced courses I highly recommend to all riders regardless of current skill:

- Total Control's Advanced Riding Clinic (totalcontroltraining.net)
- SoCal Supermoto (socalsupermoto.com)
- MotoVentures Level 2 (motoventures.com)
- American Supercamp (americansupercamp.com)
- Yamaha Champions Riding School (ridelikeachampion.com)
- Motorcycle Safety Foundation's Circuit RiderCourse (msf-usa.org)
- California Superbike School (superbikeschool.com)

I have completed 21 different courses since I started riding six years ago, many numerous times. The biggest lesson I've learned is how much I still don't know. Each breakthrough I've had as a rider was during another motorcycle course or by practicing what I was taught during the course. Education is a life-long journey. Those on the Road to Mastery are seekers of knowledge, have a beginner's mindset, and are always looking for ways to improve. The riders on the wide-open trail rely on luck, mistakenly believing they won't be put into a sketchy situation where the possibility of crashing is very high.

One of the best ways to improve your riding is to take a course on a dirt bike. Three of the courses listed above have dirt elements to them. I have attended SoCal Supermoto seven times, American Supercamp, and MotoVentures three times. I learned how to stay relaxed while sliding around and how to feel what it's like to go in and out of traction yet stay loose on the handlebars. Each one taught me valuable lessons and all of them drastically improved my street riding.

The day after I attended MotoVentures for the first time, it started raining while I was riding my sport bike home from work. I hit a patch of gravel in a turn and my tires started to slide. Normally, I would have chopped the throttle completely off, looked down at the ground, and tensed up my arms—likely causing me to crash. Instead, I did what I was taught and practiced during the course: I kept a steady throttle, stayed loose with my arms, and allowed the suspension and tires to do their job and find traction throughout the corner. I made it through with no issues, other than a mini-heart attack.

If you want more of a reason to seek out dirt bike practice, let's look at what the best riders alive do—they practice in the dirt. Moto Grand Prix racing is the highest level of racing of all, where the best riders face off at 20 tracks around the world. The current world champion is Marc Marquez. He has won three out of the last four years and practices in a variety of dirt environments to improve his abilities during the off-season: flat track, supermoto, and supercross, to name a few.

Nine-time world champion Valentino Rossi has his own personal dirt ranch for practice called Rossi Ranch (valentinorossi.com/en/). These are just two examples, but any professional racer will tell you that dirt bike training is mentally and physically beneficial for your riding. If you want to seriously improve your skills, keep taking advanced-level courses and be sure some of them involve the dirt. Jake Gagne, who is a professional superbike racer, is also extremely skilled in the dirt and is an instructor for American Supercamp. Be sure to tell him I said "Hi" when you attend the course!

What you will learn from all these courses is what will separate you from the majority. The tools you will gain will be far greater than those possessed by the average rider. You could have one year of riding experience with four courses under your belt, and with practice, you could be a more proficient rider than someone who has been on the easy path for 15 years. It all comes down to what you are willing to do to in order to improve your skills. Staying on cruise control down a four-lane highway may be easy, but you're never going to improve. Get into more training and see for yourself what you've been missing.

Once you take a course and you spend time practicing what you've learned, keep the possibility open to retake the course again in the future. For most people, your cup of understanding may have been filled up very quickly the first time around, and when you go back a second or even a third time, you will have more room to take in additional information, especially if you put in the time to practice what you've learned on your own.

A few times now, I had the light bulb come on by taking the same course for a second time; I was less nervous, I knew what to expect, and I had real-world experience of how the techniques taught applied to my riding. In addition, you now have another day to practice and get feedback from the instructors who will provide insight on aspects of your riding you may not be aware of. If there aren't numerous courses available, keep open the possibility of retaking the same course, especially if you get a new bike or take an extended period of time off from riding. This is common for many riders who have to deal with harsh winters. Each riding season would be best started by attending a course on your personal motorcycle to get back into the swing of things.

CHAPTER 6

THE BRAKES

If there were one skill I would encourage you to practice and master, it would be proper use of the brakes. Specifically, the front brake, since it has most of the braking power. When you start to squeeze the front brake, the weight of the motorcycle starts to move forward. The front suspension compresses and the weight is transferred onto the front tire, pushing it harder into the ground, providing more traction. This is why the front brake is more powerful than the rear brake and the reason why your front brake technique needs to be mastered.

A National Highway Traffic Safety Administration (NHTSA) report on accidents in 2015 revealed that 54% of motorcycle riders killed involved multiple vehicles and 46% were single-vehicle accidents. In the multi-vehicle accidents, a portion involved intersections where the rider was unable to avoid another motorist. In the single-vehicle accidents, many of those crashes involved the rider misjudging a corner and going wide at the exit.

It is amazing how much misinformation and myth there is regarding the front brake. I hear people say to not use the front brake because it will cause you to crash and to only use the rear brake for street riding. That if you touch the front brake, they claim, you're going to flip over the handlebars; that if you apply the brakes in a turn, you're going to crash. I can't help but cringe. Like any other control on the bike, it's how you use it.

The front brake should be your best friend. You should know how to use the front brake to slow you down, stop your motorcycle quickly in case of an emergency, and decrease your speed going into a corner. You should be afraid to ride your motorcycle if the front brake were somehow disconnected. I wouldn't ride around my neighborhood without my front brake; it's that important.

In my book *MotoJitsu Master Riding Program*, there are stopping drills at each belt level that get progressively more difficult on the way up to Black Belt. In White Belt, the basic level, you're required to stop in less than 25 feet at 20 miles per hour. When you start practicing Blue Belt, the speed remains the same but now you have to stop in less than 18 feet. Brown Belt requires stopping in less than 18 feet at 25 miles per hour and at Black Belt, it's stopping in less than 15 feet at 25 miles per hour. The reason I put fast stopping into the program was because of the importance the front brake has not only for stopping quickly but also with your overall confidence while riding.

Having front brake confidence gives you the ability to not be nervous going through an intersection where a car could blow through it. It prevents you from freaking out when approaching a downhill corner and will allow you to remain confident heading into a blind corner or out on an unfamiliar road, especially if you learn trail braking. Mastering the front brake needs to be a priority and will happen with consistent time set aside to practice.

As you're getting more miles under your belt and developing your own style of riding, ask yourself this question: can I stop at any moment while riding? It doesn't matter if it's at 70 miles per hour on the highway, in the middle of a turn up in the mountains, or in a grocery store parking lot while it's raining. Can you stop whenever you want and maintain control? If not, I encourage you to make more time to practice using the brakes and attend a higher-level course that can show you how to use the brakes effectively, like Total Control's Advanced Riding Clinic (totalcontroltraining.net) or Yamaha Champions Riding School (ridelikeachampion.com). These courses will go over, in depth, how to use the brakes in both straight-line stopping and while in a turn.

Having the ability to stop whenever you want, correct a mistake while turning, or adapt to a fallen tree branch as you go around a blind corner will enhance your riding confidence and lower the risk of crashing. I hope you're encouraged to not only learn how to use the brakes but also practice until the correct technique is second nature.

CHAPTER 7

MINDSET

As a motorcycle rider, you have to understand that you're the smallest motorized vehicle out on the public roads. You're the least seen and have the most risk out of everyone who's around you. If this is foremost in your thoughts every time you get on your bike, it will put you in the right frame of mind and remind you that your safety is directly related to the choices you make.

When I first started riding, I had to stop and swerve around cars at least once a week because of driver negligence. I thought all drivers were crazy, no one is paying attention, and I started to develop a negative attitude for every car out there. This is a common mindset for riders on the wide-open trail. It wasn't until I started taking more courses that I realized many of the stupid things drivers were doing weren't in fact their fault. The driver didn't cut me off on purpose, I was simply riding in their blind spot; that fast stop I did wasn't necessary, I was just traveling 15 miles per hour over the speed limit and following too closely.

Often there are things you could have been doing to reduce the chances of a sketchy situation from happening in the first place. You can cover your controls when going through intersections, look both ways when going through a green light, slow down with heavier traffic, look further ahead, and be more aware of the cars around you.

It's a good practice to check your mirrors every three or four seconds, to have an escape route in mind, and to not block yourself in while in traffic. Be sure to stay out of blind spots, predict areas with less traction and avoid them, and don't ride outside your comfort zone. Again, your safety is dependent on the decisions you make at every moment while riding.

I challenge you to seek out errors in your judgment and actions before placing the blame on others, and you will see your attitude and riding transform for the better. I understand there are situations where you're doing everything correctly and another motorist may still do something stupid. However, do your best to reduce the likelihood of that happening with good judgment. Ask yourself if there is a way you can make yourself more visible to the drivers around you? Is there a lane that's open next to you? What's the traffic looking like up ahead? Is there someone driving erratically coming up behind you? Why did this person beep their horn at you? Are you going too slow or too fast? Do they see something you're not aware of? Is there something wrong with your bike?

If you practice looking for errors in your behavior first, you will be less likely to develop a negative mindset toward other motorists and will ride with far less stress. The overall message is to have a mindset of improvement and to realize that there is so much more you're unaware of that cannot be picked up from more miles on the bike alone. More courses, more books to read, more practice to do, and more videos to watch, then repeat. It's a life-long pursuit, not a one-and-done experience.

The idea is to get your skill and judgement very high and to not take excessive risks. If you want to push the pace or explore your limits, don't do it on the public roads. Get into another course, attend a track day, or find a big, empty parking lot to gradually test the limits of yourself and your bike. This is why I either attend another motorcycle course or visit the local track at least once a month to get my adrenaline fix.

CHAPTER 8

GIVING BACK

Now that you've picked out or upgraded your motorcycle gear, selected a bike that will allow you to meet your goals, are making time to practice, and are seeking to attend additional courses, you're going to notice your skills improving dramatically. Your nervousness will lessen as your confidence increases. At this point, I'm sure you've met tons of other riders along your journey. If you haven't already done so, find yourself a mentor—someone you can rely on, practice with, and who is honest regarding your progression.

Since I started riding, I've had mentors with the same passion to learn and a talent for sharing their experience. Finding a mentor will keep you motivated to stay on the Road to Mastery. There will be times you feel you're not improving quickly enough or are still very nervous when riding; this is normal and expected to happen. A mentor can put things into perspective and keep you focused on the goal. After all, iron sharpens iron and only a diamond can cut a diamond. Even top-level athletes have coaches—taking the time to find yours is paramount.

The most satisfying feeling I get is when I receive an email saying that one of my videos was the reason why a rider has upgraded from riding in regular jeans to riding pants with protective armor inside, bought a full-face helmet instead of a half helmet, delayed buying a new exhaust in order to take an additional motorcycle course, or are out practicing MotoJitsu with other riders. The amount of comments, direct messages, and emails I get from riders telling me how I have influenced them onto the right path is so overwhelming that I'm often brought to tears. I never would have thought my videos would be so powerful as to inspire change in such a positive way.

I received an email recently from a new rider asking me this very thing: how could she inspire others? She doesn't have a YouTube channel or social media presence. She hasn't been trained in public speaking and is quite shy. She told me she feels uncomfortable talking with strangers and often keeps to herself when out practicing or while on group rides. She felt she couldn't do anything to inspire others because of her lack of experience.

I told her that by her example she is encouraging others to follow her path. I explained that every time you ride three blocks down the street to practice in a parking lot, you're taking another step in the right direction and people will notice. Every time you show up for group rides fully geared up, you're making it known to everyone that you value and understand the importance of gear. Every time someone asks you about your riding and you mention the course you've been through or the one you're about to attend, it makes an impression. When you chat about the latest motorcycle book you've read or YouTube video you watched, or mention the confidence you gained practicing MotoJitsu, you're illuminating the path to mastery for others.

I told her she doesn't have to have a title to be a positive influence on others. She doesn't have to be smart or an amazing rider, she doesn't have to have the coolest bike or the best gear. She doesn't need to give speeches or approach others giving lectures. If there's one tip I would give, it is to remember this: people will more readily follow your footsteps than your advice.

I was in the Marines for 11 years. For four years, I was a Marine Corps Drill Instructor, transforming civilians into Marines, and on my last year of that tour, I was a Drill Instructor Instructor, teaching Marines how to become DIs at Drill Instructor School. One of the most fundamental and powerful lessons I learned was to lead by example in everything.

If you cannot properly tie your boots, what right do you have to punish a recruit for the same mistake? If you cannot keep your uniform pressed and cleaned, you don't have the authority to correct someone else's. If you are not pushing yourself to get into excellent physical shape, how can you correct a recruit for not doing the same? If you do not have the moral courage to do the right thing when no one is looking, you should not be disciplining a recruit for copying the same behavior.

By your example, the people around you will either have a good example of what to do or a good example of what not to do—it's your choice. Almost every morning when I was teaching at Drill Instructor School, I would iron my uniform. I would measure my chevrons to ensure they're in the exact position and scan for any imperfections. I would brush my boots, clean off my desk, and always make sure my entire office was always in the highest level of order. The space I occupied was a reflection of myself. In addition, I would always ask fellow instructors I worked with to look me over, to see if I missed anything or overlooked an important detail.

Day after day, week after week of going through their morning routine of cleaning the schoolhouse, among other administrative tasks, more students would notice what I was doing. It didn't take long for them to start to ask for advice. How do I make my uniform look the way it does? How do I keep my shirt from wrinkling up throughout the day? What tricks have

I learned to polish my shoes or study for an upcoming exam? What insight could I provide to help increase their total number of pull-ups or to lower their three-mile run time?

So it is with motorcycle riding, I told her, and you don't have to say a word. You wear full gear each time you ride, you practice multiple times a week, you keep taking higher-level courses, and people will approach you asking for advice. I don't go up to people and mention my YouTube channel or books. I don't walk up to a new rider and start explaining how to improve their cornering or low-speed confidence.

While out riding, sometimes I would be following someone else and others might be following me. My years of attending courses and practicing my skills were getting noticed, especially since I was on a huge adventure bike keeping up with the sport bikes, often with a passenger. I would start to get questions on how I'm able to ride at a certain pace, or where I learned to execute a certain maneuver.

If you're on the Road to Mastery, this will start happening to you as well. Your skills will shine like a flashlight in the night. When you're asked about how you're able to do a U-turn so easily or about your confidence in the twisty roads, go above and beyond what's expected. Don't just say, "I've been practicing," tell them what you practice and the insights you've gained. Explain the courses you have been through, your experience while there, and even give them the website to look up. Your enthusiasm and passion will be so contagious that others will be drawn to you like gravity.

The more comfortable you get, the more you should seek out opportunities to help other riders. If there's an opening to meet up with a fellow rider and share some tips, do it. Take time to meet with others, answer questions, reply to text messages, and answer phone calls. Celebrate when your new riding buddy purchases a higher-quality jacket or boots. If a friend gets signed up for another motorcycle course, show up to support him or her. Make it a big deal when people are continuing on the right path. It all comes back to leading by example and providing that positive mentorship.

The golden rule says to treat others the way you would like to be treated. This also applies to society; behave in a way you would like others to behave. You want others to be kind and respectful, so demonstrate it yourself. Want other riders to wear gear and spend more time practicing? Make sure you do so first. Ghandi said be the change you want to see in the world, and it's true in all aspects of riding as well.

By your example, others will either know what to strive for or to avoid. Lead other riders on the Road to Mastery. Just be prepared—this journey isn't popular for many riders. There will be doubters, naysayers, and others who will try to discourage you every step of the way. I get made fun of for practicing in a parking lot, wearing full gear when it's hot outside, and attending the same course multiple times. Keep in mind that the ones who are making fun also cannot do anything I can do on the bike, so the old saying is true: haters gonna hate. The reason this negative feedback doesn't discourage me is because no one who is doing better than me has anything negative to say. Quite simply, haters don't come from above.

I was emailed once saying the Black Belt drills on my website were so easy that they could do them on a bad day. I replied with a request for a video of them performing each one of the drills. What did I get in response? Silence. When it comes to actually proving what you can do on the bike, the keyboard cowboys disappear.

Remember, you will be going against the grain, against what some other riders think you should be doing. Peer pressure is a powerful force and can be used in a positive or negative way, like anything else. It's up to you as to which path you want to be on: the one where people are barely good enough to get from work to home without crashing, or the one where riders are confident in any situation, ready to respond to whatever may happen without a hint of anxiety.

If all of this sounds good but you are still not sure what you could personally do to help others get onto the Road to Mastery, lend them this book or get them a copy as a gift. Sometimes only the smallest nudge is needed to correct someone's direction.

GREG WIDMAR

Greg, the author of *MotoJitsu Master Riding Program*, is committed to inspiring riders to wear full gear, take courses, and practice in order to reduce crashes on the public roads.

He's created over 300 motorcycle videos, available on his YouTube channel "MotoJitsu." The videos include cornering techniques, fear management, track riding tips, low-speed control, and much more. Greg shares insights he has acquired as a Total Control Instructor and from attending 21 motorcycle courses since 2013.

Printed in Poland
by Amazon Fulfillment
Poland Sp. z o.o., Wrocław